Andrew Brodie Basics

LET'S DO HANDWRITING

FOR AGES 7-8

with over **100** reward stickers

- Structured practice of handwriting strokes
- Extra tips on style and tidiness
- Regular progress checks

Published 2014 by Bloomsbury Publishing Plc
50 Bedford Square, London, WC1B 3DP

www.bloomsbury.com

Bloomsbury is a registered trade mark of Bloomsbury Publishing Plc

ISBN 978-14729-1025-7

First published 2014
© 2014 Andrew Brodie
Cover and inside illustrations of Martha the Meerkat and Andrew Brodie © 2014 Nikalas Catlow
Other inside illustrations © 2014 Steve Evans

A CIP catalogue for this book is available from the British Library.

10 9 8 7 6 5 4 3 2 1

Printed in China by Leo Paper Products

This book is produced using paper that is made from wood grown in managed, sustainable forests. It is natural, renewable and recyclable. The logging and manufacturing process conform to the environmental regulations of the country of origin.

To see our full range of titles visit **www.bloomsbury.com**

BLOOMSBURY

Notes for parents

What's in this book

This is the third book in an exciting new series of *Andrew Brodie Basics: Let's Do Handwriting*. Each book features a clearly structured approach to developing and improving children's handwriting, an essential skill for correct spelling and effective written communication. Check the handwriting style used at your child's school as there are slight variations between schools. The style used in this book reflects the most popular one.

The National Curriculum states that during early Key Stage 2 children should use the diagonal and horizontal strokes needed to join letters but they recognise that some letters should remain unjoined at this stage. They increase the legibility, consistency and quality of their handwriting: they attempt to keep downstrokes of letters parallel and equidistant, and they ensure that lines of writing are spaced so that the ascenders and descenders of letters do not collide. Enjoying the practice in this book will help your child to achieve all of these skills.

How you can help

Make sure your child is ready for their handwriting practice by checking that their chair and table are of appropriate heights so that they are comfortable and can reach their work easily. They should be able to place this book flat on a desk or table and the work area should be a well-lit uncluttered space.

Your child should place the book at an appropriate angle so that their handwriting is clearly visible to them. If your child is left-handed, the book will need to be turned to the opposite angle to that used by right-handed people: it is essential that they can see their work, rather than covering it with their hand as they write.

Martha the Meerkat

Look out for Martha the Meerkat, who tells your child what to focus on ready for the progress check at the end of each section.

Andrew Brodie says…

On some pages there are further tips and reminders from Andrew Brodie, which are devised to encourage your child to self-check their work.

When your child does well, makes sure you tell them so! The colourful stickers in the middle of this book can be a great reward for good work and a big incentive for future progress.

The answer section

The answer section at the back of this book can be a useful teaching tool: ask your child to compare their handwriting to the exemplars shown on the Progress Check answer pages. If they have written their letters and words correctly, congratulate them, but if they haven't, don't let them worry about it! Instead, encourage them to learn the correct versions. Give lots of praise for any success.

There are a few letters that all start in the same way as the letter **c**.

Copy the letters carefully.

c   c   c   c

o   o   o   o

Now try smaller versions of the same letters.

c   c   c   c

o   o   o   o

Practise joining the letters c and o together.

co   co   co   co

Make a long line of joined letter c.

ccccccccccccccc

Now practise these joins:

ac   ac   ac   ac

co   co   co   co

ca   ca   ca   ca

Andrew Brodie says...

Don't forget to use slope joins very carefully and to leave clear gaps between the pairs of letters.

Practise joining the letter o using a bridge join.

oc oc oc

oa oa oa

Make a long line of joined letter o.

oooooooooooooooooooooo

Now try these.

oo oo oo oo

oa oa oa oa

oc oc oc oc

Follow the patterns below.

oa oc oo oa oc oo
oa oc oo oa oc oo

Andrew Brodie says...

Don't forget to use bridge joins very carefully and to leave gaps between the pairs of letters.

All the joins on this page are bridge joins.

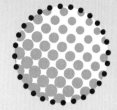

Practise these letters. They are both started in the same way as a letter c.

d   d   d   d

g   g   g   g

Now try smaller versions of the same letters.

d   d   d   d

g   g   g   g

Write these words as neatly as you can.

do   do   do   do

good   good   good

dog   dog   dog   dog

cod   cod   cod   cod

Practise these words. Make sure you leave the correct gap between the words.

good dog   good dog   good dog

Some letters on this page join with slope joins and some with bridge joins.

Andrew Brodie says...
Don't forget to leave gaps between the words.

5

Copy the letters carefully.

S s s s

e e e e

Now try smaller versions of the same letters.

s s s s

e e e e

Look at this letter e.

e e e e

We use this letter e when we need to use a slope join.

Notice how to join from o to e.

code code code

goes goes goes

does does does

soda soda soda

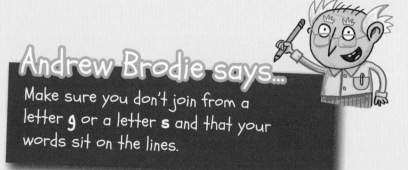

Andrew Brodie says...

Make sure you don't join from a letter **g** or a letter **s** and that your words sit on the lines.

Letter **s** starts like a letter **c** but then goes back on itself.

Letters m, n and h

Practise letters m and n.

m m m m

n n n n

Now try smaller versions of the same letters.

m m m m

n n n n

Write these words as neatly as you can.

man man man

can can can

gang gang gang

Letter h is like a letter n but it has an ascender.

h h h h

Try these words.

ham ham ham

hose hose hose

chose chose chose

Copy each pair of joined letters three times, as neatly as you can.

ac   ca   co   oc   oa   no   mo   ho   so   ce

Write each of these words five times.

ace

made

name

some

home

Can you control your writing? Copy the sentence carefully onto the wavy lines.

A good dog came home.

A good

Now write the twenty-six letters of the alphabet very neatly on the wavy lines.

a b

8

More tall letters

Copy the letters carefully.

l l l l l

b b b b

Now try smaller versions of the same letters.

l l l l

b b b b

Practise joining this pair of letters together.

bo bo bo bo

Try some more joins.

la la la la

le le le le

Write each word five times, as neatly as you can.

lane   lane   lane
bend   bend   bend
bang   bang   bang
able   able   able

Andrew Brodie says...

Don't join from letter **b** and remember to leave gaps between the words.

Joining to b, h or l

We use slope joins to join to letters **b**, **h** and **l**.

All the joins on this page are slope joins. Use a slope join to reach the top of the tall letter then come down again.

Practise joining these letters together.

al   al al

ab   ab ab

ah   ah ah

ch   ch ch

cl   cl cl

Now try these words.

all   all all

ball   ball ball

hall   hall hall

call   call call

cable   cable cable

choose   choose choose

Write this sentence as neatly as you can.

A dog had a ball.

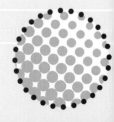

10

Letters v, w and u

 These letters of the alphabet are consecutive. That means they come one after the other

Letters v and w are very similar to each other.

V v v v

W w w w

Now try smaller versions of the same letters.

v v v v

w w w w

Practise these words. We use a bridge join to join from a letter v or w.

van van van

saved saved saved

waves waves waves

Look at how to write a letter u. We use a slope join from a letter u.

u u u u

Write these words as neatly as you can.

usual usual usual

sums sums sums

Andrew Brodie says...
Don't forget that letters which have ascenders are taller than the other letters, and that the letter g has a descender, so goes through the line.

Letter r

Letter **r** is like the first part of a letter **n**.

We use bridge joins from a letter r.

ro   ro ro

re   re re

rl   rl rl

Now practise these. Leave clear gaps between the pairs of letters and between the words.

ro rv re   ro rv re   ro rv re

rl rb ra   rl rb ra   rl rb ra

crew   crew crew

draw   draw draw

brown   brown brown

crown   crown crown

arrange   arrange arrange

Write this sentence really carefully.

I drew a good drawing.

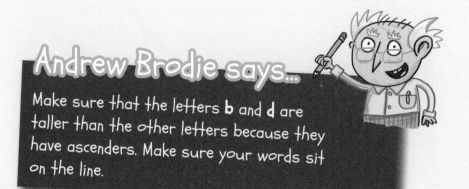

Andrew Brodie says...

Make sure that the letters **b** and **d** are taller than the other letters because they have ascenders. Make sure your words sit on the line.

Letter t

We use slope joins from a letter t.

tr *tr tr*

ta *ta ta*

to *to to*

Now practise these. Leave clear gaps between the pairs of letters and between the words.

to te ta *to te ta to te ta*

train *train train*

treat *treat treat*

tall *tall tall*

talent *talent talent*

gates *gates gates*

boats *boats boats*

Write this sentence really carefully.

I am taller than my brother.

Letter t is quite tall but not as tall as letters b, d or l.

13

Write each pair of joined letters three times, as neatly as you can.

lu bu vu wu ru tu ul ub uv ur

Write each of these words five times.

blue
tube
view
north
south

Can you control your writing? Copy the sentence carefully onto the wavy lines.

The north coast is close to here. The north

The sea is a deep blue colour. The sea

Letter **k** has an ascender.

We use slope joins from a letter **k**.

k k k k k

Now practise these. Leave clear gaps between the pairs of letters and between the words.

ka ke ki ka ke ki ka ke ki

ko ku ky ko ku ky ko ku ky

cake cake cake

koala koala koala

kangaroo kangaroo kangaroo

backup backup backup

Write this sentence really carefully.

That girl has taken two cakes.

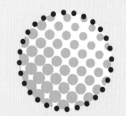
Andrew Brodie says...
Make sure that the letters **l** and **k** are taller than the other letters because they have ascenders. Don't forget to leave gaps between the words.

Letters i, j and y

Letters **j** and **y** both have descenders.

Practise letters i and j. Notice that letter j goes through the line because it is a descender.

Now try smaller versions of the same letters.

i i i i i
j j j j j

Write these words as neatly as you can. We use a slope join to join from a letter i but we don't join from a letter j.

icicle
joiner
juice

Practise letter y. The letter y goes through the line because it is a descender.

Write these words as neatly as you can.

jolly
juicy
jealous
jelly

Letter p

Letter **p** has a descender.

We don't join from a letter p.

p p p p

Now try smaller versions of the same letter.

p p p p

Now practise these. Leave clear gaps between the pairs of letters and between the words.

pa pe pi pa pe pi pa pe pi

po pu po pu po pu

apple apple apple

goalkeeper goalkeeper goalkeeper

peaches peaches peaches

repeat repeat repeat

ripple ripple ripple

Write this sentence really carefully.

The jelly was pink and purple.

Andrew Brodie says...

Remember not to join from a letter **j** or a letter **p**.

17

Letter f

We can join from a letter f using its crossbar.

f f f f

Now practise these. Leave clear gaps between the pairs of letters and between the words.

fa fe fi fo   fa fe fi fo   fa fe fi fo

farm   farm farm

offer   offer offer

faster   faster faster

famous   famous famous

fantastic   fantastic fantastic

Write this sentence really carefully.

The farmer milked forty cows.

Andrew Brodie says...

Make sure that the letter f goes above the line and through the line.

Letter q

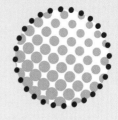

We do not join the letter q to the letter u.

 q q q

Now practise these. Leave clear gaps between the pairs of letters and between the words.

qu qu qu

quick quick quick

quiet quiet quiet

quite quite quite

quiz quiz quiz

question question question

request request request

Write this sentence really carefully.

All the children worked quietly and quickly.

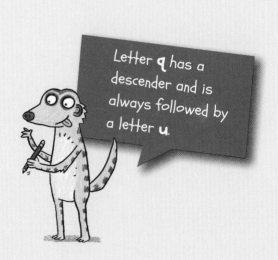

Letter **q** has a descender and is always followed by a letter **u**.

Copy the lines of letters three times, as neatly as you can.

qu fa fe fi fo ry ya jo ok ki

Write each of these words five times.

fork
jelly
quickly
quietly
fireworks

Can you control your writing? Copy the sentences carefully onto the wavy lines.

It is difficult to keep jelly on a fork.

I heard quite a funny joke.

Letter x

In this book we join to letter x but not from it.

 x   x   x

Now practise these. Leave clear gaps between the pairs of letters and between the words.

ox ax ix   ox ax ix   ox ax ix

box   box box

boxes   boxes boxes

fox   fox fox

next   next next

sixty   sixty sixty

fixture   fixture fixture

Write this sentence really carefully.

The next football fixture is on Saturday.

Letter **x** is made with two
lines that cross each other.

Letter z

In this book we join to letter **z** but not from it.

z z z z z

Now practise these. Leave clear gaps between the pairs of letters and between the words.

az iz   az iz   az iz

jazz jazz jazz

fizz fizz fizz

amazing amazing amazing

zebra zebra zebra

gazing gazing gazing

zoo zoo zoo

Write this sentence really carefully.

I was gazing at the amazing zebra in the zoo.

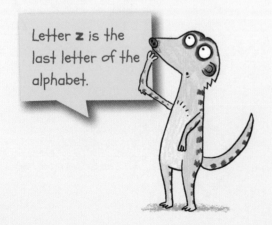

Letter **z** is the last letter of the alphabet.

The whole alphabet

There are twenty-six letters in the alphabet.

Practise the sets of letters.
Look carefully to see which letters don't join.

abcde   abcde

fghij   fghij

klmno   klmno

pqrst   pqrst

uvwxyz   uvwxyz

Now write the whole alphabet as neatly as you can.

abcdefghijklmnopqrstu

vwxyz

Now try writing the alphabet as quickly as you can.

23

Alphabetical order

Copy each of these words very carefully using your best handwriting.

alligator alligator
baboon baboon
chimpanzee chimpanzee
donkey donkey
elephant elephant
fox fox
giraffe giraffe
hyena hyena
iguana iguana
jellyfish jellyfish
koala koala
lion lion
monkey monkey
newt newt
octopus octopus
puma puma
quail quail
rabbit rabbit
shark shark
turtle turtle
under under
viper viper
whale whale
xylophone xylophone
yak yak
zebra zebra

> The words on this page are in alphabetical order.

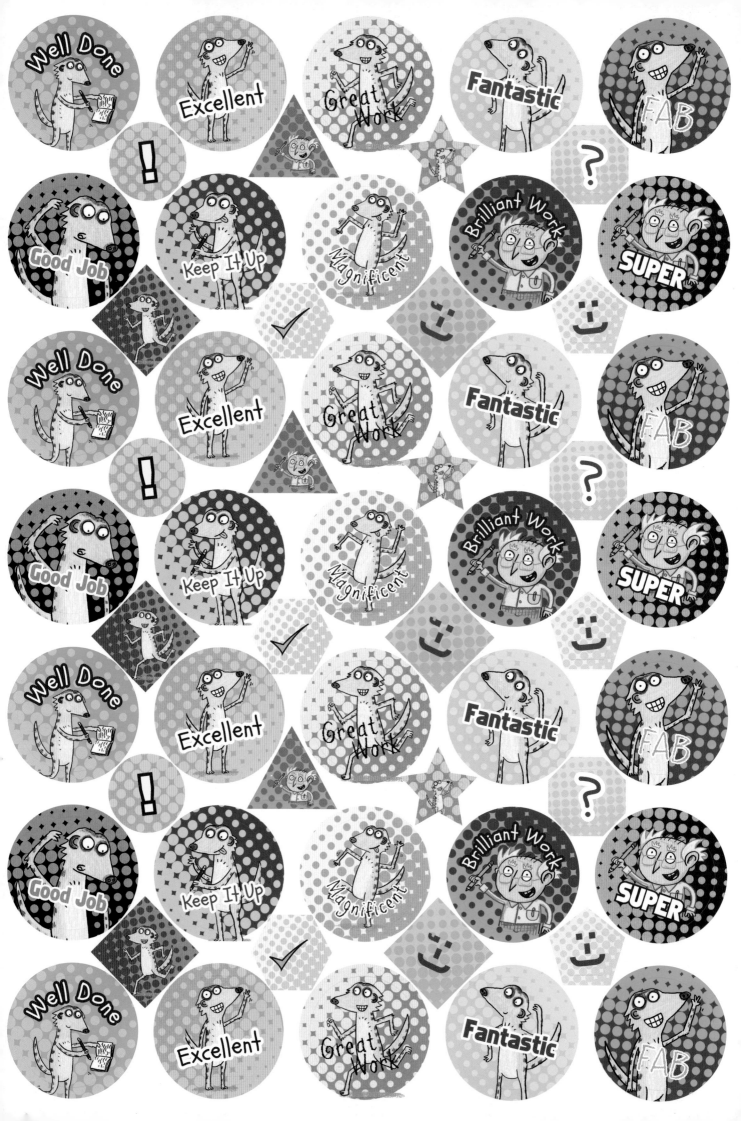

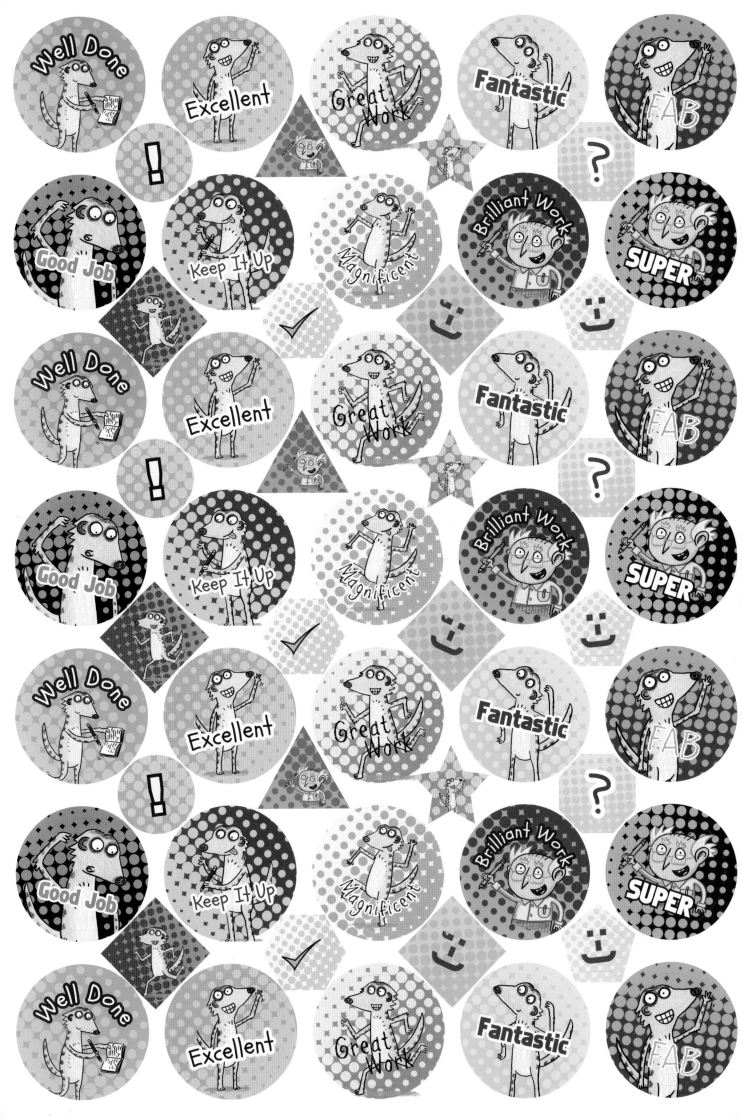

Alphabetical order

ice   umbrella   duck   parrot   kettle   apple
hurry   oven   cotton   golden   nettles   shell
year   feather   water   xylophone   bear   monster   jelly
town   ladder   earwig   rusty   zoo   queen   vase

Write the words in alphabetical order. Make sure you form your letters properly and write really neatly.

a

b

c

d

e

f

g

h

i

j

k

l

m

n

o

p

q

r

s

t

u

v

w

x

y

z

Copy the lines of letters three times, as neatly as you can.

ax   ex   ox   ix   ux   zo   iz   ze   az   uz

Write each of these words five times.

fuzzy
boxed
faxed
sixty
existing

Can you control your writing? Copy the sentences carefully onto the wavy lines.

There are twenty-six letters in the alphabet.

I fixed the broken ruler.

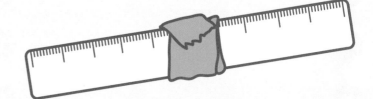

Capital letters A to E

Copy the letters carefully, then write some more.

C

Write the names of the countries.

Algeria Algeria Algeria

Brazil Brazil Brazil

Canada Canada Canada

Denmark Denmark Denmark

England England England

Capital letters are used at the beginnings of names and places.

Andrew Brodie says...

Remember that capital letters are as tall as letters with ascenders and that they are never joined.

27

Copy the letters carefully.

F F F F

G G G G

H H H H

I I I I

J J J J

Write the names of the countries.

France France France

Germany Germany Germany

Honduras Honduras Honduras

Italy Italy Italy

Japan Japan Japan

Andrew Brodie says...
Make sure that your letters sit neatly on the line.

Capital letters are used at the beginnings of the names of countries.

Copy the letters carefully.

K K K K

L L L L

M M M M

N N N N

O O O O

Write the names of the countries.

Kenya Kenya Kenya

Latvia Latvia Latvia

Malta Malta Malta

Norway Norway Norway

Oman Oman Oman

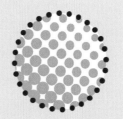

29

Copy the letters carefully.

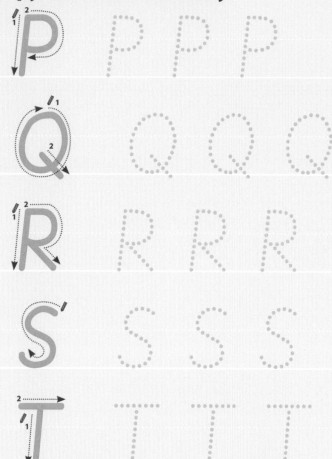

P P P P P

Q Q Q Q

R R R R

S S S S

T T T T

Write the names of the countries.

Portugal Portugal Portugal
Qatar Qatar Qatar
Russia Russia Russia
Spain Spain Spain
Turkey Turkey Turkey

Capital letters are also used at the beginnings of the names of people.

Copy the letters carefully.

Write the names of the countries.

Uganda Uganda Uganda

Vietnam Vietnam Vietnam

Western Sahara Western Sahara

Yemen Yemen

Zambia Zambia

Andrew Brodie says...

Did you notice that there is no country starting with the letter X?

31

Write each pair of letters five times.

Aa Zz Ll Yy Vv Bb Gg Ee Jj Qq

Write the days of the week in order.

Saturday   Wednesday   Monday   Friday
Sunday   Thursday   Tuesday
Monday

Write the months of the year in order.

March   August   November   January   April   September
October   February   May   July   June   December

1 January
2
3
4
5
6
7
8
9
10
11
12

Numerals 0 to 4

Copy the numbers carefully.

0   0   0   0

1   1   1   1

2   2   2   2

3   3   3   3

4   4   4   4

Now practise smaller versions of the numbers.

0   0   0

1   1   1

2   2   2

3   3   3

4   4   4

Numerals 5 to 9

Can you write numbers quickly and neatly?

Copy the numbers carefully.

5 5 5 5

6 6 6 6

7 7 7 7

8 8 8 8

9 9 9 9

Now practise smaller versions of the numbers.

5 5 5

6 6 6

7 7 7

8 8 8

9 9 9

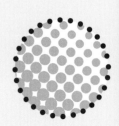

Andrew Brodie says...

Make sure that every number is the same height.

Copy the pound sign carefully.

£

Copy the dollar sign carefully.

$

Now try the euro sign.

€

Write the money signs again, but this time smaller.

£

$

€

Andrew Brodie says...

£ and $ signs only need two strokes. Make sure you keep each sign the same height.

Practise pound signs, dollar signs and euro signs.

35

Questions and exclamations

Practise the exclamation mark.

Practise the question mark.

Now try smaller versions.

? ! ? !

Copy the questions and exclamations.

How old are you?

What time is it?

Today is Friday!

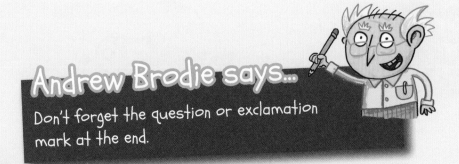

Andrew Brodie says...

Don't forget the question or exclamation mark at the end.

Speech marks

Speech marks are also called inverted commas.

Speech marks are used to show when somebody speaks. Look at this example:

"It is a nice day today," said Tom.

Copy these spoken sentences.

"What day is it today?" asked Jasdeep.

"I think it is Tuesday," replied Tristan.

"How old are you?" asked Jasdeep.

"I am eight years old," replied Tristan.

Copy this spoken sentence.

"Good work!" said the teacher excitedly.

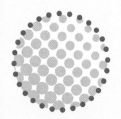

Andrew Brodie says...

Speech marks are quite small and curve inwards slightly. There are speech marks before the spoken words and after the punctuation at the end of the spoken words.

**Write each row of numbers three times,
as neatly as you can.**

28 146 52 365 625 799 17 75 190 500

28 146

Write these amounts of money very carefully.

£2.46   £3.50   £4.07   £8.99   £10.50

Copy the questions and write the answers.

"How long is it to your birthday?" asked Tariq.

"Only six days!" replied Nadia happily.

Short rhymes

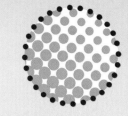

Copy these rhymes using your best joined handwriting.

Later today,
I'm going to play.

Did you notice the apostrophe in **I'm**? It's used to show that a space and the letter **a** have been missed out.

Let's fly to the moon,
We're going quite soon.

How good is your pencil control? Trace this square really carefully then draw one of your own. You will need to use a ruler.

We usually start each line of a rhyme with a capital letter.

Longer rhymes

Don't forget that we start each line of a rhyme with a capital letter.

Copy these rhymes using your best joined handwriting.

Isn't it funny,
That when it's quite sunny,
The butter is soft
And the honey is runny?

Isn't it strange,
That when there is rain,
Most of it goes
Straight down the drain.

How good is your pencil control? Trace this triangle really carefully then draw one of your own. You will need to use a ruler.

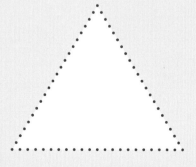

Conversation

Don't forget that we need speech marks when we write a conversation.

Copy the conversation carefully.
You can add some extra sentences at the end if you want to.

"What would you like for your birthday?" asked Mum.

"Nothing much," I replied.

"I have to get you something!" she exclaimed.

"I would like a new bike and a new scooter," I said.

How good is your pencil control? Trace this rectangle really carefully then draw one of your own.

Andrew Brodie says...

Make sure you use a ruler to draw shapes with straight lines.

Short story

Copy the story carefully. You can write some extra sentences at the end if you want to.

Yesterday morning I woke up very early. The sun was shining brightly. I looked out of the window and saw the new swing in the garden. What surprised me, though, was the fact that somebody was already swinging on it!

How good is your pencil control? Trace this circle really carefully then draw one of your own. You may need to use something circular to draw around.

Andrew Brodie says...

Make sure your circle is perfect.

Handwriting tips

By now you know lots of tips for good handwriting

Copy out the tips in your very best handwriting.

Capital letters and letters with ascenders should be taller than other letters.

All letters should sit neatly on the writing line.

Letters with descenders should pass through the writing line.

Most letters should join to the letters that follow them.

Punctuation marks should be written in the correct places.

Neat handwriting looks really good and is much easier for people to read!

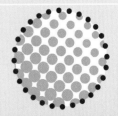

43

Copy the rhyme in your very best handwriting.

There's a hooter on my scooter,
And a bell upon my bike.
I can make a lot of noise,
For that is what I like.

Copy this conversation neatly.

"When is the next train due?" asked the man.
"At about three o'clock," replied the woman.

Use your best handwriting to copy the beginning of this short story.

The train pulled out of the station and we
were on our way. I thought the journey
was going to be boring but all of a sudden
something very strange happened.

ANSWERS

Talk about the progress checks with your child, encouraging him/her to match each one with the completed versions shown here.

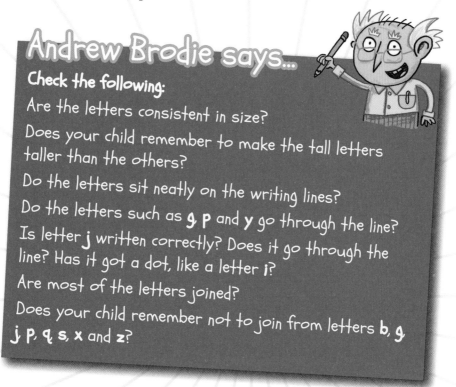

Andrew Brodie says...

Check the following:

Are the letters consistent in size?

Does your child remember to make the tall letters taller than the others?

Do the letters sit neatly on the writing lines?

Do the letters such as **g p** and **y** go through the line?

Is letter **j** written correctly? Does it go through the line? Has it got a dot, like a letter **i**?

Are most of the letters joined?

Does your child remember not to join from letters **b, g, j p, q s, x** and **z**?

Progress Check 1

Copy each pair of joined letters three times, as neatly as you can.

ac ca co oc oa no mo ho so ce
ac ca co oc oa no mo ho so ce
ac ca co oc oa no mo ho so ce
ac ca co oc oa no mo ho so ce

Write each of these words five times.

ace ace ace ace ace ace
made made made made made made
name name name name name name
some some some some some some
home home home home home home

Can you control your writing? Copy the sentence carefully onto the wavy lines.

A good dog came home.
A good dog came home. A good dog came home.
A good dog came home.

Now write the twenty-six letters of the alphabet very neatly on the wavy lines.

a b c d e f g h i j k l m n o p q r s t u v w x y z
a b c d e f g h i j k l m n o p q r s t u v w x y z

8

Write each pair of joined letters three times, as neatly as you can.

lu bu vu wu ru tu ul ub uv ur
lu bu vu wu ru tu ul ub uv ur
lu bu vu wu ru tu ul ub uv ur
lu bu vu wu ru tu ul ub uv ur

Write each of these words five times.

blue blue blue blue blue blue
tube tube tube tube tube tube
view view view view view view
north north north north north north
south south south south south south

Can you control your writing? Copy the sentence carefully onto the wavy lines.

The north coast is close to here. The north.

The north coast is close to here.

The sea is a deep blue colour. The sea

The sea is a deep blue colour.

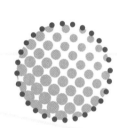

14

Copy the lines of letters three times, as neatly as you can.

qu fa fe fi fo ry ya jo ok ki
qu fa fe fi fo ry ya jo ok ki
qu fa fe fi fo ry ya jo ok ki
qu fa fe fi fo ry ya jo ok ki

Write each of these words five times.

fork fork fork fork fork fork
jelly jelly jelly jelly jelly jelly
quickly quickly quickly quickly quickly quickly
quietly quietly quietly quietly quietly quietly
fireworks fireworks fireworks fireworks fireworks

Can you control your writing? Copy the sentences carefully onto the wavy lines.

It is difficult to keep jelly on a fork.

It is difficult to keep jelly on a fork.

I heard quite a funny joke.

I heard quite a funny joke.

20

Copy the lines of letters three times, as neatly as you can.

ax ex ox ix ux zo iz ze az uz

ax ex ox ix ux zo iz ze az uz
ax ex ox ix ux zo iz ze az uz
ax ex ox ix ux zo iz ze az uz

Write each of these words five times.

fuzzy fuzzy fuzzy fuzzy fuzzy fuzzy
boxed boxed boxed boxed boxed boxed
faxed faxed faxed faxed faxed faxed
sixty sixty sixty sixty sixty sixty
existing existing existing existing existing existing

Can you control your writing? Copy the sentences carefully onto the wavy lines.

There are twenty-six letters in the alphabet.
There are twenty-six letters in the alphabet.

I fixed the broken ruler.
I fixed the broken ruler.

26

Write each pair of letters five times.

Aa Zz Ll Yy Vv Bb Gg Ee Jj Qq

Aa Zz Ll Yy Vv Bb Gg Ee Jj Qq
Aa Zz Ll Yy Vv Bb Gg Ee Jj Qq
Aa Zz Ll Yy Vv Bb Gg Ee Jj Qq
Aa Zz Ll Yy Vv Bb Gg Ee Jj Qq
Aa Zz Ll Yy Vv Bb Gg Ee Jj Qq

Write the days of the week in order.

Saturday Wednesday Monday Friday
Sunday Thursday Tuesday

Monday Tuesday Wednesday Thursday
Friday Saturday Sunday

Write the months of the year in order.

March August November January April September
October February May July June December

1 January
2 February
3 March
4 April
5 May
6 June
7 July
8 August
9 September
10 October
11 November
12 December

32

47

Write each row of numbers three times, as neatly as you can.

28 146 52 365 625 799 17 75 190 500

28 146 52 365 625 799 17 75 190 500

28 146 52 365 625 799 17 75 190 500

28 146 52 365 625 799 17 75 190 500

Write these amounts of money very carefully.

£2.46   £3.50   £4.07   £8.99   £10.50

£2.46   £3.50

£4.07   £8.99   £10.50

£2.46   £3.50

£4.07   £8.99   £10.50

£2.46   £3.50

£4.07   £8.99   £10.50

Copy the questions and write the answers.

"How long is it to your birthday?" asked Tariq.

"How long is it to your birthday?" asked Tariq.

"Only six days!" replied Nadia happily.

"Only six days!" replied Nadia happily.

Copy the rhyme in your very best handwriting.

There's a hooter on my scooter,
And a bell upon my bike.
I can make a lot of noise,
For that is what I like.

There's a hooter on my scooter,
And a bell upon my bike.
I can make a lot of noise,
For that is what I like.

Copy this conversation neatly.

"When is the next train due?" asked the man.
"At about three o'clock," replied the woman.

"When is the next train due?" asked the man.
"At about three o'clock," replied the woman.

Use your best handwriting to copy the beginning of this short story.

The train pulled out of the station and we
were on our way. I thought the journey
was going to be boring but all of a sudden
something very strange happened.

The train pulled out of the station and we
were on our way. I thought the journey
was going to be boring but all of a sudden
something very strange happened.